I STILL BELIEVE

• SONDA JONES •

I STILL BELIEVE

A Battle between the Heart and Mind

TATE PUBLISHING
AND ENTERPRISES, LLC

Published by Tate Publishing & Enterprises, LLC
127 E. Trade Center Terrace | Mustang, Oklahoma 73064 USA
1.888.361.9473 | www.tatepublishing.com

Tate Publishing is committed to excellence in the publishing industry. The company reflects the philosophy established by the founders, based on Psalm 68:11,
"The Lord gave the word and great was the company of those who published it."

Cover design by Joana Quilantang
Interior design by Shieldon Alcasid

Published in the United States of America

ISBN: 978-1-68270-768-5
1. Biography & Autobiography / Women
2. Religion / Christian Life / Inspirational
16.02.01

ACKNOWLEDGMENTS

I WOULD LIKE to dedicate this book to my beautiful daughters, who have lived life with me through many hard times and also through many victories. Together we have learned to trust God in a way we never thought possible. Girls, I am so proud of you for never giving up. I pray you will always seek God in every aspect of your lives.

Next I want to dedicate this to my amazing parents, who have been by my side. Mom, I am so thankful for the many prayers you have offered for me. You have always been there for me. You have taught me to always believe. Dad, I will always remember what you said after the most tragic thing in my life had occurred. You said, "This is what faith is all about." Wow, what a blessing you both are to me!

I also want to dedicate this book to my wonderful pastors, who are also my uncle and aunt. Ray and Jean, thank you for believing in me. Thank you for never giving up on John and me. You both are such a blessing, not only to me but also to all the people you minister to each and every day. Don't ever quit doing what you do. God is so good!

INTRODUCTION

I OFTEN WONDER, "How in the world can I ever write a book?" I would never have thought about doing that until I went to a convention and had the pleasure of sitting next to a beautiful female minister. As we were eating lunch, we shared stories about our lives. On the last day of the convention, she asked me, "When are you going to write a book?" That totally shocked me. Is my story truly one that people would read? As I continued to process all this in my mind, I did a whole lot of praying and talking to God. I told him if he would give me the words, I would write them down. This book is really not about me or my story, but it is about Christ living in me and giving me the strength to continue to live this life here on this earth. So as I start this journey, I pray you will be touched by the Holy Spirit, and He will give you the strength to live.

1

I WAS BORN on October 2, 1962, to my wonderful parents, Raymond and Gaylene Hunt. I am the youngest of three girls. I was very blessed to be raised in a Christian home. We went to church every time the doors were open. Although we had our family squabbles, like any other , I was always surrounded by a prayerful mother and a loving father . My parents held high standards and prioritized morals. There were times I felt they were too strict so much so that I missed out on a lot of things, but now that I am older, I am so glad and proud of the way I was raised. I had Jesus in my heart at a very young age; I have never known life without Him.

It was fun growing up with two sisters. Since I was the "baby," everyone thought I was spoiled. Of course, I disagree. They did love me and took care of me. I was strong-willed and very protective of them. I would put up a fight to protect my family, and because of that, nobody ever got away with teasing or hurting them.

I was a very active and athletic child. I loved to play football, basketball, and volleyball. I also loved swimming, bicycle riding, and anything else that required me to be outside. I was so determined that when I set my mind to do something, I would do it such as when I tried to run as fast our car. One day my mother let me out of the car on a dirt road just so she could prove me wrong. Needless to say, I was really disappointed when I found out I couldn't run that fast. It was probably a good thing I broke my arm the summer after first grade. That put a little fear in me and kept me a little safer in my life. I decided right then that I didn't like pain.

I attended public school until I reached the ninth grade, when our church opened a private Christian school. I graduated from high school in 1980. Soon after graduation, I got my first job at BC Clark Jewelers. I learned all about fine china, crystal, and flatware. Three and a half years later, I was promoted to the jewelry department and furthered my education in diamonds and diamond grading, and now I am a registered jeweler. This is the only job I have ever had, and I have thoroughly enjoyed working there all these years

I never dated much because I believed God would bring me the right person so I wouldn't have to search around for him. I wanted someone who was appealing to the eye—you know, tall, dark, and handsome (that was every girl's dream). But most of all, I prayed for a man who loved the Lord with all his heart. I wanted to marry someone who was not ashamed of the Gospel.

I had my eyes on such a young man who had started attending my church in 1977. His name was John Edward Jones Jr. He became a Christian and served the Lord with all his heart. I'm sure I was too young for him to notice me. Back then, I was only fourteen years old while he was eighteen . Wow, I was practically a baby in his eyes! He dated another girl in the church, yet I still held out hope and wondered how or when he would notice me.

As the years went by, I watched John as he grew in the Lord. He was not raised in church like I was. He started serving the Lord after he graduated high school. The thing about John was that he never did anything halfheartedly. When he received Christ as his personal Lord and Savior, he was a changed man: He started coming to church every time the doors were open (I remember one time he walked to church because his car wouldn't start). He studied the Bible and loved God more than anything. He wanted to see the church grow and would go out into the streets to spread the Good News to people. He was never ashamed of Christ. He even put an intercom system in his car and drove up and down the streets shouting "Jesus loves you!" That would embarrass most people but not John. He felt that his calling in life was to preach the gospel. He also attended Bible college to better his knowledge about the Bible.

My aunt and uncle, Pastors Ray and Jean, were youth pastors in our church. They have always been a great support to John. Sometimes they drove him home after church and talked to him for hours. They were so excited to see the growth in John that they encouraged him to continue walking with the Lord.

John's mother was a beautiful Christian woman. His father, however, was a little different story. I would never judge his walk with God, but he was a hard man. He was never happy about John becoming a Christian and never supported the "call" John had in his life. This made it difficult for John to go home at night; he would be all excited about what the Lord was doing in his life, but when he gets home, there'd be no show of support from his father. You know how it is. We all want our parents' approval, which really shouldn't have been hard to get in John's case because it wasn't like he was going out and getting drunk or into trouble; he was usually at a youth rally or at a church event.

Eventually, Pastors Ray and Jean asked John to be a leader in the youth group. He studied the Bible and preached to the youth. He loved it and was always very humble and appreciative of his position. His ultimate goal was to minister to people wherever he was.

In October 1979, John asked Ray and Jean what they thought about him asking me out on a date. Of course, having known me all my life, they thought that would be a great idea. So on October 11, 1979, we had our first date! It was pretty amazing to me. The man of my dreams finally noticed me! I was the happiest girl in the world. That very moment, I knew he would be the man I would marry one day.

Things were pretty amazing back then. I led praise and worship in church, and John preached to the youth. I knew deep in my heart that ours was a relationship created by God and that nothing would ever stand in the way of us serving Him.

On August 14, 1981, John and I were married. We faced our challenges as all young couples do. We both worked hard at our jobs and really tried to live the life we were called to live. We attended church together and we wanted to be used by God as his faithful servants.

As I've said before, John really wanted to see the church grow. He also was one who had a heart for the lost and broken. So it was no surprise that a few months after we were married, he went to a pastor in our church. He wanted to talk to him about taking the bus and picking up kids in nearby apartments to bring them to church. He also wanted to talk to the pastor about going out and ministering in different places and churches (our pastor sent young ministers out to preach on different occasions to give them experience in the ministry).

That conversation changed the course of our lives; however, it wasn't in the way that we'd initially thought.

If I had known what that conversation would do to my husband, I would never have wanted him to go through with it. The pastor told him that if he went out and ministered in other places, all the people would follow him (John) and not himself. That hurt John in a way that I probably will never understand.

John had so much respect for this man. If there was one thing John was taught at home, it was respect. It was never his intent to hurt anyone or to steal anyone's ministry. John was a strong, tough man, but his heart was tender. He decided that if this was what a *pastor* thought about him, he didn't want to have anything to do with the ministry. It took many years for him to get over this.

I was always taught to put my trust in God and not in a man because man will fail you every time. I think because he didn't have a strong godly upbringing, he didn't know how to handle that conversation. From that day on, we stopped going to that particular church, and I struggled for many years for John to take us to church at all.

2

When I was a little girl, I noticed when women went to church without their spouses. My father always took the whole family to church, so I didn't understand why these women went alone. I told myself that when I get married, I will never go to church on Sunday without my husband. Now, after John's conversation with that pastor, what was I going to do? I wasn't used to not going to church. I really felt like I was sinning whenever I didn't attend.

I remember all the times I begged John to take me to church. Sometimes if I screamed loud and long enough, he would break down and take me. I know from many years of experience that it is almost impossible to live a Christian life without attending church. There is a reason the Bible says, "Not forsaking the assembling of ourselves together..." (Heb. 10:25, KJV). It takes people of like faith to lift each other up. Listening to the Word of God and applying it to our daily lives will help keep our faith strong. I know you don't have to go to church to be saved, but it sure helps .

Shortly after John and I were engaged, we got the news that my grandfather (James L. Grantham) was diagnosed with myeloma . He had a small sore on his hand. The cancer grew so quickly that it totally disfigured his hand in a matter of months. He heard about new forms of treatment in Mexico and decided to go there in hopes of finding a cure. He stayed there for several weeks, but nothing seemed to help. He returned home to undergo surgery (he was going to have his hand amputated).

We have always been a family of faith, so naturally all of us prayed for God to heal him. In the midst of my grandfather's illness was when John and I got married. Shortly after the wedding, my grandfather underwent yet another surgery— this time, to remove the rest of his arm. I have never in my life seen anything so awful. By then a huge tumor had grown under his arm. It was about the size of a grapefruit. It was a wide open sore and oozed out pus from the infection. He spent the end of his life in the hospital. I remember when John and I once visited him. The minute we got off the elevator, we could smell the open sore. If the devil and death had a smell, that was what I imagined it to smell like. I can't even explain how horrible it was. In April 1982, my grandfather passed away.

Just a few months prior to my grandfather's death, I found out that my cousin Jeff had cancer. He was fifteen years old. Oh my, what an amazing young man he was! He was an incredible piano player and a gifted singer as well. He was a true example of a young man living for Christ. He and I were always close growing up, and when I started dating John, he and Jeff became buddies. Jeff had always looked up to John and wanted to be like him. It was so cute. He even wanted to dress like him. I remember that one time when Jeff was sick, we bought him some jeans and a shirt like John's . He couldn't wait to wear them.

Jeff's cancer started with a pain in his knee. His parents (Uncle PD and Aunt Esther) took him to the doctor and found out that Jeff needed to have his leg amputated. First, my grandfather and now my cousin...How can this be? No matter how hard we prayed, it didn't help. Jeff was advised to undergo surgery and then chemotherapy. But the cancer spread to his kidneys and then to his lungs. It was so sad to see such a young man go through this devastating illness. Jeff had his sixteenth birthday in February 1983 and in July passed away. It is so hard to understand why these things have to happen, but somehow God gives us the strength to make it through difficult times.

In 1985, I found out I was pregnant. We were all so happy. I spent the morning of my days off with my grandmother. This was going to be her first great-grandchild. We talked about the baby and many other things. We laughed together, cried together, and prayed together.

During my pregnancy, however, we found out my grandmother (Ruth Grantham) had cancer. She was in and out of the hospital but eventually ended up in a nursing home. I remember that at Christmastime the doctors called the family in because he felt she would soon be gone. I went out into the hall to talk to God and to tell Him that she couldn't die until she saw my baby. It was a promise I felt God had made me. Sure enough, she got a little better and lived one more month after the baby was born. I was so happy she was able to hold her first great-granddaughter.

3

My first daughter, Rachel Lynn Jones, was born in January 8, 1986. She came into this world really fast. I woke up at 6:00 a.m. and started hurting really bad. I didn't realize I was in labor until around 8:00 a.m. We jumped in the car but didn't know if we would make it to the hospital in time. We sped through the school zones, trying to get to the hospital as fast as possible.

By the time we got there, I knew the baby was coming. I was rushed to the delivery room, and at 8:39 a.m., she was here. Rachel looked so much like her daddy that people would ask me if I was her mother. But there was no doubt about that. After all, *I* was the one pregnant with her and was sick every day for nine months; my feet and ankles were so swollen that they were about the same width as my knees. Yes, I *am* her mother! Ha-ha!

December 15, 1988, our second daughter was born. Unlike Rachel, Heather Renee Jones took forever to come into this world. I thought that since Rachel came so fast, Heather would too. But oh no, that wasn't the case! I labored *all day* with her. Finally at 10:26 p.m., she came into the world. It was a good thing that I already had Rachel because I decided I wasn't having another child after having had such a long, hard delivery with Heather. Heather didn't look as much like John as Rachel did, but somehow she looked enough like Rachel that as they got a little older, people would ask me if they were twins. They were three years apart. I do have to admit that they look similar but not enough for them to look like twins.

John and I loved our little girls. They were so beautiful, and we knew we were blessed to have happy and healthy kids. Early on, we focused on raising them to believe in the Lord. Even though John did not take us to church very many Sundays, I always took them on Wednesday nights. I made sure they learned about Jesus in their classes at church. I'm not sure it was the smartest thing I have ever done, but I never broke my vow that I would not go to church on Sunday without my husband.

John and I worked hard and provided as best we could for our family. Our kids grew up knowing right from wrong, having been raised with good morals and values. They would tell you that we were too strict and that they were sheltered, but I think now that they are grown up, they are glad about how they were raised. I think as parents we need to be stricter and not let our kids control us. The Bible does say, "Train up a child in the way he should go: and when he is old, he will not depart from it" (Prov. 22:6, KJV). I believe in the Bible and in the fact that all its promises are for me.

As the years went by, John and I had our ups and downs. There were many days of us fighting and disagreeing with each other. Ours was probably not much different from most marriages that are not centered on God. Somewhere along the way, I stopped begging so much about going to church as a family. I decided to turn it all over to God. It wasn't easy though.

John also secluded himself from everyone else. He really didn't like people at all. He said that 95 percent of the world was stupid. (I'm not sure that he *wasn't* right.) The people he worked with called him the Intimidator, and I absolutely hated that. John was never a bad man, but somehow I never felt he was living the life God called him to live; however, I am so glad that God has mercy on us and that He never gives up on us. No matter how long it takes or how far we drift away from Him, He is always one step away. This is proven in Romans 10:13 (KJV), which says, "For whosoever shall call upon the name of the Lord shall be saved." God's mercy can rewrite your past.

As the years went by, the girls gradually entered their teenage years. They did very well in school, and both decided they would attend college after high school graduation. I am thankful that God watched over them and kept them from danger. I think they realized that I would never give up on God to somehow wake their daddy up and change his heart.

4

WHEN HEATHER WAS sixteen, she went through a spell of great depression. There was a lot of confusion going on in her head. She totally shut down and stopped talking to us. This went on for several weeks, and we really started worrying about her. One evening, I asked her if I needed to get her some help. She said yes. (We were all sitting in the living room when this conversation took place.) I looked over at John and said, "We need to pray."

I had relied on prayer all my life. I hadn't always seen the results I wanted to see, but I never gave up and never stopped praying. I knew we would have to seek professional help, but I decided that we were going to pray first. We all stood in the middle of the living room and joined hands. As a family, we prayed and asked God to give Heather peace of mind. This whole situation scared John; and I think for the first time in many years, he realized he was going to have to trust God. He loved his girls more than he did his own life. He never wanted them to be hurting. From that very moment, John changed.

The next day was not just another Wednesday as John wanted to go to church with us. We were all sitting in the same row, and I was so happy we were all singing and worshiping together. There was a special speaker that night at church. She was from Oral Roberts University. I don't remember exactly what she preached, but I noticed that at the end of the service Heather went up to pray. I didn't mind because I knew that if anyone could help her, it would be God. Heather and I didn't have much conversation after church, but in the upcoming days, I saw positive changes in her.

As I look back on those days of Heather's depression, I wondered why she went through that in the first place. She had always been a happy, loving child. She had lots of friends and everyone loved her. Could it have been because of her (our) family life? Could it have been because of all the bickering going on in the house? Could it have been because of prejudices she saw in her father? And I knew that although she wanted to please me and John, her parents, she wanted to make decisions for herself—decisions she probably thought would separate her from her family. Could this battle in her mind ever be healed?

Because of the prayer that night in the living room, God started changing John and Heather. Our communication became more open . John became a happier person; and because of that, Heather became comfortable coming to me to ask about how we felt about different things in her life. I was always the one the girls would go to first, and then I would talk to their daddy about it.

One of the conversations I had with Heather involved her asking me how we felt about her dating a young black man. She said he was a Christian and promised me, "Mom, if you would ever meet him, you would love him." If she had ever asked that question before, I know John's response would have been "Absolutely not!" It's not that he hated black people or anything like that, but he was taught that the whites and the blacks shouldn't mix. I think all of us were taught to think that way. Maybe not in a verbal way but in an unspoken, understood way. We were pretty firm about that too. But now, after everything our family's been through, we were trying to be more open-minded and to talk about whatever Heather wanted to talk about.

Much to my surprise, when I talked to John, he said that he was okay with it. It seemed that God was really working on John as he started loving people more. To him, it didn't matter what color they were anymore; he loved them. When Jeremy came to pick Heather up on their date, he treated us with the utmost respect. I have never seen a young man so kind and respectful toward us. After he and Heather left for their date, John looked at me and said, "Red and yellow, black and white...They are precious in

His sight." This was a huge statement coming out of from John's mouth.

John was right though. God doesn't look at what color we are or what denomination we belong to. He only looks at our heart. He cares about what we are on the inside. He cares that we love Him with all our heart, soul, mind, and strength and that we love our neighbor as we do ourselves. As time went by, we still had challenges with Heather's mental state, but God continued working as we continued to put our trust in Him.

5

After John decided to serve the Lord again, so many things started to change. It started with him wanting to see Pastors Ray and Jean. Even though they were my aunt and uncle and we saw them on occasion at family gatherings, he would try to avoid talking to them about God, but he knew they had never given up on him.

Anyway, he couldn't wait to see them. They were pastoring in a little church in Okemah, Oklahoma. It was about an hour and a half away from our house. We called and made an appointment to meet with them. I'm telling you John was *so* excited to tell them that he was back to serving the Lord that we made it there in record time.

When we arrived, they were so happy to see us. We talked for several hours and even had communion with them. They prayed over us and asked God to guide us. Our marriage became stronger than ever, and our family was whole again. I was extremely happy because I had waited many years for this to happen.

Next, John wanted to apologize to certain people. The main person on his mind was the pastor who had hurt him many years before. He made a special effort to go to the church and tell the pastor he was sorry for holding a grudge against him. He then went to several family members and friends to apologize for his bad attitude and wanted their forgiveness. He felt so much better after he had done these things. I believe healing comes after we forgive others. When you carry unforgiveness in your heart, it will weigh you down, and you might not even realize it. The Bible says if we don't forgive our brother, then God will not forgive us.

John started to seek God for direction in his life. He started to "hear" the call in his life again. He took us to church every Sunday and Wednesday. As much as we could, we drove all the way to Okemah for church on Sundays. It wasn't just that; John became the friendliest person I had ever seen. I have always loved people and crowds unlike John; he had truly separated himself from other people. All that was happening was a true miracle. This wakeup call changed John for the rest of his life.

Everywhere we went, we made friends—whether it would be the waiter at a restaurant or even the greeter at Walmart. Loving people like Jesus loves us will change you. As Christians, we are supposed to strive to become like

Christ. It is your choice to allow God to change you and clean you up. God doesn't make us serve Him; He gives us the choice to do it. Just like in Adam and Eve's case, He gave us a free will. We too can choose life or death.

John really wanted to do something different with his life. He had been a welder for over twenty years and was getting tired of it. It was way too hot, especially in the summer months. So he prayed that God would show him a new direction.

One thing John was good at was drawing. He was a true artist. When he was in high school, he drew some amazing pictures and wanted to pursue a career in commercial art. He reproduced the cover art of a magazine and drew a picture of a werewolf. He also drew the most incredible picture of King Kong I had ever seen. It was so good that he made a silk screen of the picture so T-shirts could be made; however, someone stole it and started making T-shirts without John's permission. He, of course, was not happy about that, so he sought out the silk screen and tore it up. (I still have the original picture though.)

John never pursued a career in art because he was always told at home, "Boy, artists are a dime a dozen." No matter what he drew, something was wrong with it. It is amazing to me how negative words can really hurt a person and can sometimes change their course in life. Through the years, John struggled with drawing, never thinking he was good enough; therefore, he stopped drawing.

Now that John's life had changed, he started praying about everything . He wanted God to use him somehow. He really wanted to quit his job and minister to people in a different way. God started talking to him about drawing again. John was such a perfectionist that he often gave himself a hard time, but he was determined to draw anyway. Shortly after, things just started happening, and I watched as God started to direct our path.

Every day, after John got home from work, he went to his room and drew. He worked for many hours on this one project. He loved drawing with a style called stippling. With this style, a picture is formed by tiny dots. He used a 000 NIB ink pen and drew thousands of tiny dots to form a beautiful picture. Drawing more dots in one area would create a shadow. I had seen only one picture drawn that way, and it was the one he drew of King Kong when he was in high school. John had the steadiest hand of all the people I had ever known. This is important because just one tiny slip of the hand might create too big of a dot or a blob on the picture and would surely ruin it.

Day after day, hour after hour, John drew until one day his project was finished. He brought the picture to me when I was sitting on the couch. I hadn't seen it in a while because he wanted it to be a surprise. It was a picture of Christ's hand with a nail pierced through the center of it and blood dripping down. I sat there staring at it. It was perfect. I knew it was a piece of art. Every tiny dot was in its place, and there was not a single blemish. I looked up at John and said, "Baby, this is perfect! Just like Jesus's love is for us. I think we should name it *Perfect Love.*" He thought that was a great idea.

What you might not understand is that I waited almost twenty-five years for John to come back to the Lord, so for John to actually finish a picture was a true *miracle.* Right then, I realized that all the years of praying were worth it. For me to see him pour his heart out to God and seek His face was the best thing that ever happened.

God will meet us wherever we are. Even after twenty-five years, God is still right there. All we have to do is call upon His name.

6

Now we had a picture but didn't have any idea what to do next. So what were we going to do? We did what we have done since John's reconciliation with God: we continued to pray and ask God for direction. We knew that if God was in this, He would open the doors we needed to go through.

We decided to start a small business. The plan was that John would continue to draw pictures, and we would sell them. He had so many ideas of what he would draw: it would all be Christian art—pictures that would illustrate scenes from the Bible. We then bought all kinds of supplies like paints, pencils, brushes, canvases, and drawing tablets; however, that was the easy part. The hard part was finding out how to market the pictures. We had one original picture so far. *Where do we go from there? How do we make prints of them?* We had no idea what to do next. But we did know how to pray, and we believed God would show us what to do.

John and I loved going to air shows. Every year, our city has one, and we'd watch all kinds of airplane stunts. One of our favorite groups to watch was the Blue Angels as they flew in perfect formations . Going to an air show with John was like reading an encyclopedia about airplanes. He loved airplanes and knew about every single one of them. He loved the old planes and could tell you what kind they were and in which war they flew.

One thing we had to do while we were there was to find the tent with all the artwork . There was one particular artist whose paintings, which displayed pictures of planes, John always looked for. We always found ourselves buying one of his prints. The artist was never there at the shows but he had someone working for him take his prints to shows and sell them ; however, on this particular year, the artist was there.

So there we were, at an air show, talking to an artist about his prints. I got to thinking, *Would he tell us how to get started on selling prints?* I was a little timid about asking him questions, but I thought this was the perfect time to do so. I said, "You have this original painting of a plane. How do you get prints to sell from the original?"

Much to my surprise, he was open and friendly about it. He not only told us the steps but also how many megapixels of a digital camera it would take to take the best picture of the original. He gave us the name of a photographer he had hired; then, he gave us the name of the print shop he went to and even told us the type of paper that he found to be the best (as to thickness) for his prints. After all that, he gave us his business card and told us that if we had any more questions to feel free to call him.

When we walked away, we were so amazed at all the things we had learned. I thought, *Could this really be happening to us?* Believing is one thing, but seeing is a whole different story. God was truly paving the way before us. Now it was our job to walk it out and get things done.

The first thing we had to do was talk to a photographer and have a digital picture of the original taken. That was easy. My cousin Tammy is a professional photographer, and I knew she would have the perfect camera to take the picture. We decided that if she would agree to it, we would give her the first limited edition (signed and custom-framed). She agreed and the next step of this project was complete! Now we needed to go to the printer. We did go to the print shop the artist told us about. The personnel were so friendly. They knew the artist we had met at the air show. They knew exactly what kind of paper to use, so all we had to do was to decide how many to print. Oh my, how things were working out! We had a picture *and* the prints.

As John and I were talking to Tammy one day, she suggested we get a website. She referred us to a gentleman named Steve, who had helped her with her website. John and I were so excited. We made an appointment with Steve and decided to meet him at a restaurant to talk things over. Steve was so interested to hear our story.

John talked with him about his life and how God was changing him. He told him how he wanted to start a business selling his paintings. He knew that God would bless the business and that he would someday be able to quit his job, travel to art shows, and maybe even go to churches to tell his story. Steve was so impressed with it all. When we showed him John's drawing of Christ's hand, he loved it. Steve looked at us straight in the eyes and said, "This is not a business. This is a *ministry*."

He wanted to be a part of this so much that he didn't even charge us for creating the website. That was another miracle! God was opening the doors we needed to walk through. Now we have a website (artfromtheheartok.com). It tells John's story and also talks about the vision he had about his artwork. We had several prints framed and decided to give some of them away to different people who had always supported us with their prayers and had never given up on us.

7

TIME CONTINUED TO fly by. Our girls were growing up: Heather was attending college in Tulsa, Oklahoma; and Rachel was in college in Edmond, Oklahoma. Rachel had been dating a young man named Tyson, and they were engaged to be married in June 2009.

John started drawing another picture. It was a crown of thorns, three nails, and a hammer lying in the sand. He planned to name it *It Is Finished.* After John turned his life around, he never got the sacrifice Christ made for us out of his head. He wanted to draw pictures that would reveal that message to others. He had finally accepted Christ's grace and mercy for him.

One day in December 2008, Heather and Jeremy had come home from college for Christmas break. Rachel and Tyson were also at the house with John while I was at work.

They were all watching TV. John got tickled and started to laugh. He was eating at the time, so he choked on his food mid-laughter. He decided to get up and go to the kitchen when all of the sudden, he passed out and fell to the ground face-first. He fell so hard that he had a carpet burn on his forehead.

Tyson ran over and turned John over on his side, and Heather called 911. She also called me at work. Before the ambulance could arrive, John came to and said he was all right. When I got home, we talked about the incident. It didn't bother him at all. He said that if he didn't wake up, he would be with Jesus and that it was fine with him. I got so mad at him when he said that because I wanted him to stay with me; I wasn't ready for him to leave me. He just thought it was funny and went on.

January 2009 came and it was pretty cold for the month. Our winters in Oklahoma were getting a lot colder. It also was not unusual to have ice storms, and this year was no exception.

Pastor Ray asked John and I to speak one Sunday morning at church and tell the people what God had done in our lives the past year. When it was my time to speak, I told the people how much stronger I was in Christ. I had been trying to read and study the Bible more than ever before. I was so happy me and John were on the same page now. It made a huge difference in our lives as individuals and as partners in marriage.

When John got up to speak, he told the people, "Love the Lord your God with all your heart, soul, mind, and strength and to love your neighbor as yourself. If we would do these two things, God would do the rest." These two commandments were so simple, but somehow we make them so hard to do. We as Christians make life so complicated. If we would only do what the Bible tells us, God will give us the strength to go through the trials of this life.

January 23 (Friday). John and I had dinner with friends.

January 24. John and I had dinner with Rachel, Tyson, and his parents. We wanted to get to know them better since Rachel was going to marry their son. We talked and enjoyed our time with them.

January 25th. It was inventory time for me at work. I left at about 7:30 a.m. John was snoring in the bed when I left. It took several hours for me and my coworkers to do inventory, but we finished at around 3:00 p.m. I was so happy (John and I were going to go to the movies if I got off early enough). When I got into the car, I called him and told him I was on my way home. He said to me, "Baby, I'm sick." I said, "Okay, we will go another day." When I got home, John was wrapped up in a blanket. I thought nothing of it as it wasn't unusual for him to act like a little baby when he was sick. He could be pretty dramatic.

January 26th. John was still sick, so he stayed home from work. I went to work and later that day we had an ice storm. It was very cold and the streets were very slick.

January 27th. John was still sick and it was my day off. I was glad I was home with him. He was coughing and had a fever and a hard time breathing. I called the doctor to see if I could get him an appointment. The weather was so bad that the doctor's office had to be closed. His doctor was on call though, so I was still able to talk to him about John. I told him of his symptoms, and he said that it sounded like RSV (respiratory syncytial virus). He said it had been going around in adults lately. He told me to give him ibuprofen and Tylenol and rotate them every four hours. I did that day and night, and John's fever broke. We went to bed; but in the middle of the night, I woke up and saw John beside the bed on his knees praying.

January 28th. John was still feeling bad and was still having trouble breathing. I called the doctor again and set up an appointment for John to see him. I drove John right up to the door at the doctor's office, let him out, and then went to park the car. I walked to the door thinking he was already in the office, but he was still outside right by the place I had left him. He could barely walk to the back row of seats in the office. I checked him in, and we waited to see the doctor.

We were called in and we sat in a little room. The doctor came in and used a stethoscope to listen to any abnormalities in his breathing. He said that he wanted John to take an x-ray. He put John on oxygen, and then to the x-ray room we went. John could barely stand up. I had no idea he was this sick until I noticed how he couldn't seem to walk. I literally had to hold his arms up while they took the x-ray. After the x-ray, we went back to the little room. The doctor came in and said, "I don't want you to argue with me, but I have called an ambulance to pick you up and take you to the hospital."

I will never forget the look on John's face. He hadn't been sick very much in his life, and now he was on his way to the hospital in an ambulance. I saw fear and concern in his eyes. I told him I would be right behind him in the car, that I would always be right by his side, and that he and I would deal with this together. Right away I called his family and mine. I wanted everyone to start praying for him.

When we got to the hospital, they looked at John's x-ray. They couldn't believe what they were seeing, so they wanted to take another one. I still had no idea what was really going on. I followed as they wheeled him to the x-ray room. I stood behind the radiologist while they were taking the x-ray. He showed me how John's right lung was totally white. They knew it was pneumonia but were not sure if there was an abscess or some kind of mass behind it. They then wanted to do a CT scan to find out for sure.

John was having so much trouble breathing that the doctor thought it would be a good idea to lightly sedate him to make him more comfortable during the procedure. We agreed and they wheeled him out of the room. They said that it would take only a few minutes and that they would come get me afterward. I called everyone again and told them what was going on. The weather was so bad that only the people who lived close could come to the hospital. I called Ray and Jean , and they tried to make it to the hospital from Okemah. They got to I-40 only to find that it had been closed, so they had to go back home. Rachel and Tyson were with me while Heather and Jeremy were at school in Tulsa. Some of the rest of my family came.

We all waited and waited and waited. We wondered why it was taking so long. No one was telling me anything. When I could no longer take it, I went to the nurses' station and asked. They pointed to the room John was in and told me that they were having a hard time stabilizing him. They said that I could go in. It dawned on me then that between his heart rate and his oxygen level, things were not looking good. John was still lightly sedated and was trying to raise himself up off the bed. I knew in my heart he was fighting. I went over, lay beside him, and talked to him. I told him that everything was going to be all right and that he was in a place where he was going to get help.

After many hours, they got him stabilized but didn't want him to be conscious because they needed him to be as relaxed as possible. He was taken to the intensive care unit (ICU) on the ninth floor. We then came to find out that his right lung was severely infected from *Streptococcus pneumoniae* (pneumococcus), the leading cause of bacterial pneumonia. There was no abscess and no mass. They took samples and found it out . Fortunately, we were told that this was common and treatable. I was sure that in a few days, he would be back with us.

8

JANUARY 29, 2009 was a rough day as we tried to keep all of John's stats up. Heather and Jeremy made it home from Tulsa. My aunt and uncle made it to the city along with friends we had in Okemah. All of our family and friends that could come came. Phone calls were made to everyone we knew to ask them for prayers. We had ministers all over the world praying. I knew in my heart that God was still a God of miracles and that John would come through this. I had prayed all my life, and God had never failed me; He has always been with me. I knew this time would be no different. I stood on the faith I had and was determined not to waver from it.

January 30 was another trying day. Things were not looking good: John had been on a respirator since the first night in the hospital. As the day went along, John's right lung collapsed. They said they would have to put a tube in it to drain the fluid. That worked for a little while, but then it collapsed again; then, they wanted to put in a larger tube. I have never seen anything like it. There were so many tubes and machines hooked up to John that I couldn't believe it myself.

Jeremy's father (Lloyd Moore) is a doctor. He couldn't believe all the things John was hooked up to. He said that it was a miracle that everything was regulated like it was. He had tubes going to his lung, oxygen tubes, medicine tubes, and machines that would show his heart rate and oxygen level. This was a day I had to cry out to God for peace of mind.

As we were all sitting in the hall, talking to the doctor, and crying because John was getting worse, God brought a song, which someone had written in our church, to my mind. The words were "I will rest in You / I will rest / I will rest in You / in the shadow of Your wings / Your love is covering / You hold life in Your hands / every dream, every plan / You are my rest." This song brought me comfort and peace.

January 31 was the hardest day yet. The lung doctor came in and talked to us. She said that John's oxygen level had been low so long that if things didn't change by Tuesday, we might want to think about unplugging all the machines. She felt that by then, John's mind would be nonfunctioning. I never thought I would be in the position to pull the plug on my husband. He was so young—only forty-nine years old.

So many things went on in my head. *This cannot be happening to me. My husband was perfectly healthy a week ago, and now I'm going to have to decide to end his life or not.* I just started praying. Certain words I had heard from a song came to my mind, and I started singing it to myself. The words went something like this: "What can I fear / when You're here with me? / Almighty God / to You I'll run / I'll never look back / my eyes on You / oh Lord, to ever hold on to You." *Oh, how I love Christian music!*

So many songs that gave me strength came to me. I remembered the times we would drive to Okemah to church and put a Christian CD in and sing all the way there. John couldn't carry a tune in a bucket, but he didn't care; he sang anyway. Heather knew her daddy loved music as well. While her daddy was in the hospital, she lay beside him with her arm across his chest, her iPod on with one earbud in her ear and the other in her daddy's . Together they listened to music.

On February 1, oh my, how the prayers went up! As the day went along, we were noticing how much John's oxygen level was going up. Heather stayed in his room all day rooting for her daddy. His oxygen levels read 85, 86, 87, 88…90, 91, 92, 93…96, 97, 98. *Yes! His oxygen level went all the way up to 98.* We were so excited. Prayers were working and we were happy.

The only time I ever left John was every other day at 4:30 a.m. to go home, take a shower, and hurry back to the hospital at around 7:00 a.m. Rachel became very sick while her daddy was in the hospital; so a lot of the time, she was at home trying to get better. She came to the hospital as much as she could but couldn't stay with us.

Heather and Jean stayed with me at the hospital day and night. They found a small room down the hall and called it their little condo. They slept there while I slept in a reclining chair right next to John. Jean stayed with him every time I left the hospital. Every time I drove back to the hospital, I prayed. When I reached the parking lot and looked up at the hospital, I said, quoting Psalm 23:4 (ESV), "Even though I walk through the valley of the shadow of death, I will fear no evil for you are with me. Lord, please deliver me from this fire like you delivered Shadrack, Meshack, and Abendego."

By February 2nd, it was just a waiting game. Second by second, minute by minute, hour by hour, day by day, we prayed that the medicine would work. The doctor had totally paralyzed John's body so it didn't have to do anything. The nurses rotated his body from side to side every few hours. My family and I started falling in love with the nurses that would take care of John. Melanie and Carolyn were our favorites. It just seemed John did much better when they were on call.

I understood some of the nurses kinda fought over him. They wanted to take care of him on their shift. I was amazed at how much the nurses loved him when they had never even met him before. That made me so happy. I told the nurses how special they were, and I knew being a nurse was their calling. Not just anyone could be a nurse. I told them that they were storing treasures up in heaven and that I was sure God was pleased with them. I believe that every person on this earth has a purpose and that God will show us what that is if we ask Him to.

February 3 was my dad's birthday. We had a lot to celebrate. This was supposed to be the day I was going to have to make the decision on whether or not to turn off all the machines. John's oxygen level had been up for the last several days, and things seemed to be looking better. He wasn't out of the woods by any means, but I didn't have to make that decision now. We celebrated my dad's 81st birthday at the hospital.

By February 4, John had been in the hospital for a week. His heart doctor visited him. They had discovered a leaking heart valve several years before all this, and we kept an eye on it every year. I asked him how his heart was, and he said that it was very strong. He said, "Give him every chance to live because his heart is strong." That gave me more hope. I felt sure his recovery was near.

On February 5, it was a rough night. Every time the nurses turned John on his right side, he had a major setback. Oxygen levels went down while his heart rate went up. Everything was going wrong. It got to the point where they couldn't even put him on his right side. Each morning, they came in and took an x-ray of his lungs. By then the infection had jumped over to his left lung. Time went by so slowly as I just watched him lie there. *How could all this be happening?* I knew in my heart that John was going to have a miracle. Too many good things had happened the last few years, so I knew it couldn't end there. I just kept holding on to my faith and refused to give up.

When I woke up on the morning of February 6, I looked over at John. I noticed that his eyes were slightly open. It kind of looked scary to me. I knew he wasn't conscious. His eyes were glassy looking. The nurse said that sometimes this happens. I asked her if we could do anything about it. She said that we could tape them shut. But when they did that, it looked even worse. There was no way I could look at him like that all day; then, they suggested we put a cloth over his eyes to cover them up. I said that it would be fine.

This was another long day. His heart rate raced too high, and his oxygen level was coming down again. We had a lot of visitors coming and going, and many people stayed in the waiting area for hours on end. I was so thankful for all the support and for all the prayers from everyone. I honestly believed that people who never prayed very much were praying now for a man they all loved. People came in every day. All of these big, burly men from John's work came in, stood at the foot of John's bed, prayed, and cried.

They talked to him and told him how strong he was and how they wanted him to get better and come back to work.

By February 7, we'd spent ten days in the hospital. My physical body was getting very tired. I wanted something to happen. I looked at John with a cloth over his eyes and at all the machines keeping him alive. It was a painful, pitiful sight. I knew John was getting weary. I felt it. I thought that maybe he was torn between going to heaven and staying here with me. I didn't know what he was feeling, but I wanted him to be peaceful and happy. *How many more days would this go on?* I held his hand and started praying and talking to him. I lay across his body and whispered in his ear , "Baby, if you want to go be with Jesus, you go right ahead and go. I will take good care of the girls. One day, I will see you in heaven."

I look back at the day in December when he passed out. I knew that day he would have been happy to leave this world. This day was no different. At that point, I left it all up to God and John. They would be the ones to make the choice. This too was another long day of waiting, waiting, waiting. I had stepped out of the room to get a late dinner when the nurses were trying to get me on my phone. I got back to the room to find John in cardiac arrest.

Carolyn was on duty at the time and was pounding on John's chest. We had agreed several days earlier that we would not resuscitate him if anything happened. I ran to him while she tried to get the doctor on the phone. I started pounding on his chest as well. The girls were right there, and so were several family members and friends .

At 9:10 p.m., John took his last breath. Screaming, falling to the floor, and crying filled the room. Emotions were so high. My girls had lost their daddy, I had lost my husband, and many others had lost a friend. At that point in my life, I just wanted the whole world to stop, but somehow that didn't happen.

9

SO FINAL, THERE I was. A widow at forty-six years old. I thought, *This can't be real. God, help me through this.* It's like my whole world went into this thick fog—so many clouds to look through. I was looking for clarity in my own mind. I had questions but no answers.

John and I never really talked about our final plans (if one of us were to die). We thought we were too young. We never even had a will made because we didn't want anyone else to raise our girls , and we just weren't comfortable writing those kinds of things down on paper. Decisions had to be made right that second—decisions I had to make without my husband.

As I sat in the waiting room with the chaplain of the hospital and everyone gathered around talking, I had to decide which funeral home I wanted to come to the hospital to pick up John's body. Oh man! I remember it just like it was yesterday. *Was it just coincidence they had just finished building a brand new funeral home minutes away from our house?* John and I talked about it as it was being built, wondering what it was going to be before the signs showed. Never in a million years had I thought that would be the day I would need their services. I decided that would be the perfect place. Next, we had to leave the hospital for the last time.

As we gathered all our belongings, my dad and Steven went into the men's room. They were discussing all that had happened. My cousin had a very difficult time dealing with the whole situation as did the rest of us. My dad, who is not a man of many words, said, "This is what faith is all about." Such a true statement that was—but one that was not easy to walk out. The ride home was very quiet. I mean, what words could anyone have said to make sense of things?

> *February 8, 2009 (Sunday).* What a day this was! My mom, dad, aunt, and uncle took me to the funeral home to make plans for John's final resting place. I would totally advise any couple who hasn't made those plans to do so. It would have been much easier on me had we done that! You will not be in the right state of mind after your partner's death to make those decisions. What kind of casket do you want? Where do you want him buried? Where and when

do you want to have the funeral? It's all too much to handle!

February 10. Monday and Tuesday were a big blur. I know many people came to the house and brought all kinds of food for the family. They were so kind and generous to us. I even had friends offer to stay at the house while we were coming and going back and forth to the funeral home so that someone would be there if we had visitors come by. I am so thankful for family and friends. I also made plans for the order of the funeral (who would sing and who would speak).

February 11. This would be the day I would bury my husband of almost twenty-eight years. It was a sad day but was also a joyous one. All the years of praying for John's soul had paid off. This life here on earth is but a vapor (James 4:14), but eternity is forever.

I remember the night before I took John to the doctor's office. He was on his knees praying. I honestly believed he would have died at home the next day if I hadn't taken him to the doctor, and somehow I think John knew something was really wrong with him. When John was sedated, he did not know if he would never wake up, but he did know where he would spend his eternity. And that brought me a lot of joy.

About three hundred people attended John's funeral. I remember the days we had very few friends (those were the days John secluded himself from people). He said to me a few months before he died, "We have lots of friends, don't we?" I replied, "We sure do!" Looking at all the people at the funeral proved that! A large group from John's work came. Many other friends and family were there. Four nurses from the hospital were there to pay their last respects. Even the greeter from Walmart was there (she never even knew our names!).

Steven, Regina, and Tammy sang two beautiful songs, one of which I remembered singing to myself at the hospital when John's lung collapsed (there is something to be said about resting in the Lord). Chad (from John's work) spoke at the funeral and talked about how much of a witness to God's Word John was at his job. He called him his missionary and friend.

Travis (from our church in Okemah) talked about John and how much he loved and would miss him. He told everyone about how John had impacted his life and that he would never forget him. He said that all who knew John would have a piece of him with them.

Sharon, my cousin, talked about John and said that she had noticed a positive change in him when we went to the last family reunion. She also talked about the beautiful picture John had drawn of Jesus's hand and how it had spoken to her. She talked about how twenty-five years of bitterness had gripped John's heart because of the rejection of man and how God's perfect love can change us if we ask.

My sweet aunt Jean also talked about John and how close she was to him from the very first time they met at church about thirty years earlier. She said that they had a special bond and that they shared their dreams with each other. She shared with everyone about how John believed in her and how she believed in him. They had a lot in common, and they encouraged each other on a daily basis. She also read the eulogy Rachel prepared—how he was her best friend, how when she was a kid she wanted to be just like him when she grew up, and how she was Daddy's little girl. She talked about how she spoiled her daddy and loved every minute of it. She said that her daddy loved God first and how much people needed a touch from God.

Next, Heather got up and read a letter she had written to her daddy. She talked about how he had helped her develop her faith—not the "baby" kind of faith that comes and goes when things were good or bad but the immeasurable amount of faith that she would continue to have after he was gone. She said that she was proud that he had kept the faith and finished his race and that she would do the same.

I then went up to the front and talked about John. I talked about how I would miss him and how I would have to rely on God to continue. I wanted

> the people to know how important it was to John that everyone have a personal walk with God.
>
> My Uncle Ray performed the service, and it was beautiful. He talked about how John had a talk with Jesus. He said that even though we didn't understand how this piece of the puzzle of life fit, we had to trust that God knew how it would . He even led the people through the sinner's prayer and said that if they wanted to repeat it, they had the opportunity.

John would have been so happy. You see, after he came back to living a Christian life, he wanted everyone he knew to follow Christ. He never wanted anyone left behind. That was the same way he felt all the way back when he was eighteen years old, and that was the way he felt the day he died. I feel sure many people were touched at the funeral.

Ray and Jean stayed with me for several days after the funeral, but I knew the day would come when I would have to face life alone. Life-changing things had happened in a matter of a few days. I really didn't know how I was going to go on or what I was going to do next.

John and I had huge plans together. We were in the prime of our lives. We had raised our girls, so it was just me and him. We had truly fallen in love again. So many years of bickering and fighting had been changed by putting God back in the center of our marriage. Remember that a three-strand cord is not easily broken. Things weren't perfect, but they were definitely better. It is a challenge being married. God will show you things you need to change about yourself if you are open to it and if you ask Him to show you.

Life is all about choices; we make them every day. Praying together will help keep one strong. I know God hears our prayers. It's clear to see how God was directing our path, opening doors we had to walk through. I also know that we live in a fallen world and that there is a devil out there ready to kill, steal, and destroy anything he can. Could this loss be a ploy to destroy me and my family? Perhaps. How would I make it on my own? I had no idea.

I have always been one to try to figure things out. I always wanted to know why things happen. In my mind, if I could answer all the questions, I would be satisfied. No matter how much I thought about it, nothing made sense. A perfectly healthy man catching the most common and most treatable type of pneumonia has his right lung totally consumed in a matter of three days, gets rushed to the hospital where he gets the finest care and $236,000.00 worth of the most powerful medicines—mixed specially just for him—poured into his body for ten days, is then put on life support, and yet eventually winds up dead! *We never even said good-bye.* It was so hard to get all that out of my mind.

10

LITTLE DID I know that the last few years of studying the Bible, going to church, and really listening to the messages and applying them to my everyday life were preparing me for what I had to go through .

I decided early on that I would never blame God for what happened. Even though John's death had shaken me, I knew in my heart that it couldn't destroy me. My heart and my mind were two different things, and I struggled between the two. A few weeks before John passed, my uncle preached about God being a good God (The scripture he read was James 1:17 and John 10:10).

No evil thing comes from God but from the devil. I remembered the message and repeated it over and over in my mind. Even though I remembered these words, I still had trouble understanding why God didn't answer my prayers concerning John's healing. I had plenty of faith and knew Jesus healed every person he touched in the Bible. God had answered my prayers many times before.

How much faith does one have to have? I believed until John took his last breath. Questions, questions, and more questions overpowered my mind at times.

What about all the scriptures in the Bible, the very ones John and I stood on? Scriptures like Jeremiah 29:11 (ESV), which says, "For I know the plans I have for you, declares the Lord, plans for welfare and not for evil, to give you a future and a hope." What about Romans 8:28 (KJV), which says, "All things work together for good to them that love God…"? Does God think this is good?

What about all the songs I had held onto in the hospital, songs that were written straight from the words of the Bible and gave me strength? What about Jeremy Camp's "You Never Let Go," which says, "And I will fear no evil / For my God is with me / And if my God is with me / Whom then shall I fear? / Whom then shall I fear? / Oh no, You never let go / Through the calm and through the storm / Oh no, You never let go / In every high and every low / Oh no, You never let go / Lord, You never let go of me"? How was I ever going to hang on?

Which battle in my mind would win: keeping my faith as I had always done or choosing to throw in the towel and forget about serving God? As always, the devil will try anything to get you to lose your faith as he thinks he has the perfect plan to try to destroy you. The one thing I knew I would have to do was to choose to live. How was I going to do that? I really didn't know.

Every night, I lay in my bed and cried out to God (and I meant cry *real tears of pain*). That was the loneliest time I had in my life. There was no one beside me to protect me. No one to hold me. No one to talk to. On the very first night after John's burial, I asked God to comfort me. And I don't mean just speaking softly to myself but out loud. The Bible says He will be my comforter, and I had to believe it. What else was I supposed to do? I needed His strength to keep living because I knew that I cannot do this alone.

Everything I had to do was so hard, but the hardest thing had to be going to church. That was John's favorite place to go. How in the world was I going to be able to sit through a service? I will tell you right now that it *wasn't* easy, but I went anyway. I bawled like a baby every time. The songs I heard were the same ones that built my faith before, but now I had a hard time believing them. The sermons had the same messages I had heard all my life—they talked about faith and how God was for me and not against me—and now I was struggling whether or not to believe them.

How was I ever going to believe these things again? How was I going to believe them for myself? Day by day, week by week, I did the same thing: I cried out to God. He gave me peace beyond my understanding. He comforted me and gave me peaceful sleep at night. I knew He picked me up and started carrying me as I was convinced there was no way I could have done all that I had *alone*.

God gave me the strength to get up and go to work. All my coworkers were so supportive, but working with others and exposing myself to people each day was challenging. Making it through the day without crying was impossible. The things people said made me so mad. They said things like "This too shall pass." *Are you kidding me!* Most people had no idea what or how I felt. I appreciated it most when people didn't say anything at all—when they just hugged me and loved me. I didn't want people to ignore me, but I needed people to love me and pray for me.

It was hard choosing life. It would have been much easier giving up, staying home every day, curling up in bed, and forgetting it all. But no, that's not what God wanted. He doesn't want that for anyone. Something deep inside me somehow just kept churning.

I tried really hard to believe God had a plan for my life. I spent many hours with my parents and talking to my aunt and uncle. I continued to go to church each week. My aunt told me about a scripture that helped change my thinking. It is found in Deuteronomy 29:29 (KJV). It says, "The secret things belong unto the Lord…" Okay, if that is what the Bible says, I would accept it. At that point in my life, I started giving all my questions to the Lord. I knew that if I was going to continue to go forward, I had to believe that scripture and accept in my heart that God knows all the answers and that I didn't have to.

I knew Rachel's wedding day was arriving soon. Her dress came in while we were in the hospital with John. This was another huge challenge we had to face. *Would we continue planning the wedding or just forget it?* Rachel didn't even want to have a wedding anymore. All her dreams of her daddy walking her down the aisle had been crushed. In her mind, she had her daddy all dressed up in his tux and dancing with her. Now all that had changed.

I tried to be strong for her and talked with her about it. I told her that her daddy still wanted her to have a beautiful wedding. I said that I didn't know how we would get through it but that we could try together. I told her I knew I wasn't her daddy and that no one would ever replace him, but I would be honored to walk her down the aisle. Heather asked her as well to walk her down the aisle. Somehow she agreed and we continued planning.

Oh, it was so hard! Living in those thick clouds made it hard to focus on what we needed to do. My parents came over every week on my day off and helped us. I know we couldn't have done it without them.

The wedding day came. We had a beautiful memorial table set up right down the front of the chapel. John's picture was on the table along with a floral arrangement that matched Rachel's bouquet. A candle was also placed on the table along with a runner that said Daddy's Girl. I was escorted down the aisle to light the candle.

All the way down the aisle, I was thinking, *Why am I the one doing this? John, I wish you were here. This is not my place.* I lit the candle; and before I could walk away, it went out. I took a deep breath, lit the candle again, and said to myself, *John, please stay here with me and help me through this.*

This time the candle stayed lit, and I walked back to meet Heather and Rachel. The bridal music started playing, and Heather and I walked Rachel down the aisle. Arm in arm, the three of us stood strong. Under the circumstances, it was the most beautiful wedding I'd ever been to. I knew John was looking down on us, smiling.

11

Another thing that I battled against was guilt. I guess guilt is part of the grieving process, but I didn't know that at that time. I never felt guilty about things like "What if I had done this or that?" and "Maybe John would still be alive if..." But every time I did anything for myself (like purchase something), I felt guilty. (It is really hard to explain.) If I tried to move forward, I felt like John moved farther away from me. It's almost like taking one step forward and then three steps backward.

I remember the day five months after John's passing. I was driving in his truck to work. There was a pair of sunglasses hanging from the sun visor. John loved sunglasses and wore them every day—you could say they were part of his wardrobe. I looked at those sunglasses every day for five months and never touched them. That day I looked at them and said, "I can wear those. John would be happy if I did." I took them down and put them on. At that very moment, I thought ,*John would not be happy if I didn't go on. He would be kicking me in the pants if he knew I would quit. John would want me to be happy and continue to live.* That very day started my healing from guilt.

Several months passed, and I felt like I was moving forward. I had been thinking about John's sermon on loving the Lord with all your heart, soul, mind, and strength. I knew I loved the Lord with all my heart, soul, and strength, but I was struggling with the mind part. *How do I love the Lord with all my mind?*

September was the time of year when several people in our church in Okemah attended a convention. This was a place where I received more healing. I was learning that healing is a process and that it takes time. Even though I had heard that all my life, it's not until you go through a traumatic situation when you really understand its meaning. This convention was a very spiritual experience, and I loved going each year.

John and I had been the two years prior . It was a place where you could go and soak in the presence of the Lord. The praise-and-worship portion was so beautiful. I could listen to the music all night. After the music would be the message. On this particular night, after the message was spoken, the pastor of the church went to the pulpit and started singing an old song I hadn't heard since I was a young child. These are the words: "Jesus, I just want to thank you / Jesus, I just want to thank you / Jesus, I just want to thank you / Thank you for being so good."

I looked at the words on the screen as he sang the song. As much as I tried to believe that God was good, I just couldn't sing the song and mean it. I knew it in my heart, but I couldn't wrap my mind around it. I totally broke down and cried. My aunt was sitting next to me. She took my hand and walked me down to the front for prayer.

As I stood there crying, a lady from the other side of the room ran to me and asked me if she could hold me. She had never seen me before, nor had I ever seen her before. She said, "I don't know your situation." She then started to pray and said, "You are not alone." She also said that when I lie in my bed at night, I would be comforted, and Jesus would give me sweet dreams. She didn't know my situation, but God did. That was true conformation that God was still with me.

The next evening, I went down to the front to pray. Just me and Jesus. I asked Him to take over my mind. I turned all my questions, all my whys, over to the Lord. As I stood there, a pastor came over to me and started to pray. A lady beside me was praying for me as well. She put her hand on my stomach. The pastor said, (which was related to the passage of scripture found in John 7:38), John 7:38, "From out of your belly would flow rivers of living water." He then said that I would have joy again, that I would speak words of life to people; then he said, "Don't be afraid to make a mistake. When God tells you to do something, do it." You must understand that these people had never seen me before and didn't know my situation. I was so excited that I couldn't contain myself. I spent the next day feeling differently.

I got home the following night and had such a strange burning sensation inside. I couldn't go to bed until 2:00 a.m. At 4:00 a.m., I woke up. I was remembering when John stood up two weeks before he got sick and told us to "love the Lord your God with all your heart, soul, mind, and strength." While lying in bed, I sensed God revealing this to me. He broke down the scripture word by word. God said to me, "The other night you turned your mind over to me…All of your questions and whys…I know you love Me with all your heart, soul, and strength. And now you love Me with all your mind."

Our minds are so powerful. God gave them to us to make choices. Like I said earlier, God doesn't make us do anything: It is our choice to serve Him or not. It is our choice to hate or to love, to be mean or to be kind. The only way we will have true peace is to keep our minds focused on Jesus.

> You will keep in perfect peace those whose minds are steadfast, because they trust in you. (Isa. 26:3, NIV)
>
> Do not conform to the pattern of this world, but be transformed by the renewing of your mind. Then you will be able to test and approve what God's will is—His good, pleasing, and perfect will. (Rom. 12:2, NIV)

December 2009 was my first Christmas without John. Since I worked in retail, my time was taken by my work. That was good because it kept me busy, and I didn't have time to think about myself. It was a very cold December and one I would never forget. On Christmas Eve, we had the biggest blizzard on record. The last few years had been very cold and we had bad ice storms, but I have never seen a blizzard in Oklahoma City.

I had to work until 5:30 p.m. and then head home. The wind was blowing so hard, and the snow and ice had been falling all day. I couldn't get my car doors open because they were frozen shut with ice. I was so thankful there was a man who helped me get in my car. I spent several minutes scraping my car and warming it up. It was a very slow process driving home—a trip that normally took twenty minutes took over two hours. I slipped and slid around and even got stuck on the sheet of ice, not able to go anywhere.

I finally made it to my house only to find the snow drifts about three feet deep in my driveway. I sat in my car, wondering how I was going to get it out of the street. There was no way I was going to leave it there all night. I got out of my car and walked to the front door. The snow was so deep and the only things I had to use to scrape it away from the door were my hands and feet. I then came to realize that I had no one to help me. John was a very strong man; and if he was there, he would have already had a path for me. The pain started all over again. My heart began to ache as I scraped the snow away from the door. With tears in my eyes, I finally made it in the house.

Losing someone so close to you is very difficult. You just don't get over it in a few months. There are so many things that remind you of that person.

I changed my clothes, got my boots on, and then headed out to clear a path for the car. That was a night I cried a lot. With every heavy load on the shovel, I cried. All the while, I thought, *Why did this have to happen to me? Life is so unfair.*

After a few hours, I was able to get my car in the driveway and then into the garage. I then realized that there will always be hard times and that it is okay to cry; tears can help wash away some of the pain. I had to remember that I can go there but that I cannot stay there. This was when I reached down deep inside of me and start praying for God to comfort me.

I am a firm believer that if we seek God, we will find Him. If I never call upon His name, I will never find comfort. As the song goes, "There is a river that flows from God above." It is my choice to believe that and jump into it. *God, please consume me! I love you dearly, Lord. You are all I need.*

12

TIME WENT BY and I found another year behind me. I continued to become stronger as the months passed. I knew God had been carrying me in His arms. I really felt by this time that God was gently putting me down so I could continue to run my race with the faith He had instilled in me.

In the spring of 2011, I had the opportunity to attend a three-day women's conference, wherein my Aunt Jean was the main speaker in New Mexico. It was an incredible trip. My aunt was an amazing speaker and ministered to all the women. I was amazed at all the different stories and life situations many of the women shared and had. My aunt prayed with the ladies as well.

There was one young lady who had just gotten out of jail that very first day of the convention. Her husband was a praise-and-worship leader in the church. She admitted she was addicted to alcohol and drugs. We prayed that God would deliver her from these addictions.

Another woman had trouble with her parents who were making bad choices. She felt she was a fake because of it all. Jean told her that she couldn't control the choices her parents made but that she could control the choices she herself made.

One other woman was having problems with her children.

Several women were spiritually, mentally, and physically tired because they were trying to be like someone else. God made each one of us different. We don't always have to struggle to be like anyone else. The person we need to strive to be like is Christ. I know that people who go to church and even have positions in the church struggle with major issues.

After having listened to all the stories, I asked God, "What do I have in common with all these women? Their stories are so different from mine. I know I have a story, but what common thread do I have that I could bond with these women and help them through their circumstances." I didn't feel my story was complete.

I thought and thought about it and then prayed about it. I asked God to show me something. I went to bed that night with all this on my mind. In the middle of the night, God woke me up and started to reveal something to me: He told me that we all have to find the seed of faith that was planted in each one of us the day we accepted Jesus as our personal Lord and Savior. The minute we ask Christ in our heart, God plants a seed of faith. Everyone has the same measure. If we exercise it, we can make it through all life's situations. Is it easy? No. But God gives us strength if we ask for it.

When we become saved, God equips us with everything we need in His Word, the Bible. We need to study and find the scriptures and then quote them out loud and believe them for ourselves.

> Renew our mind daily. (Rom. 12:2, NIV)
>
> Greater is He that is in you, than he that is in the world. (1 John 4:4, NIV)
>
> I can do all things through Christ who strengthens me. (Phil. 4:13, NKJV)
>
> I know the plans He has for me is to prosper, to give me hope and a future. (Jer. 29:11, ESV)

It doesn't matter what your situation is—whether it is a death in the family, a divorce , a sickness, family problems, addictions or any other situation—God gives us the faith to believe we will make it through. He gives us the opportunity to make the right choices. He doesn't make them for us. Here we are again, choosing whether or not to trust Him or to give up.

That next day, Jean asked me to share my story with the ladies and tell them what God had revealed to me. I said that even though we were going through different struggles and situations in life, our common thread was *faith*. If we dug down deep, we will find it, and we will be conquerors through Christ, who strengthens us.

We become stronger and stronger each day if we continue to seek God. I was so happy that I had the opportunity to go on that trip, to support my aunt with prayers, and to share my story with others.

13

DO YOU REMEMBER the story I wrote in the beginning of this book (the one about Heather's depression, the miraculous story that changed John's life)? Well, May 8, 2011, was a very special day: Heather and Jeremy were getting married. They had dated a couple of years in high school, and then they both attended Oral Roberts University (ORU) in Tulsa, Oklahoma, for four years. God helped Heather continue her education after her daddy's death. It was an extremely difficult time for her being away from me and still having to deal with that great loss.

God truly helps us if we ask him to. There were many nights when she called me crying. Somehow I found myself being strong for her. It was so hard being a parent who had to be away from her child during difficult times. Just like how I had to go forward, I had to encourage her to keep going. She did an amazing job. She even wrote her story in a letter to her daddy, and it was published in the ORU yearbook. Both of my girls still have days when they struggled, and there will always be those days. I am so proud of them for finishing school and, most of all, for the faith they have in God.

Preparing for Heather's wedding was not quite as difficult as planning Rachel's. I just kept thinking, Time does heal, so we would make it through this day as well. Heather struggled with knowing her daddy would not be there to walk her down the aisle. That is a feeling I never had to deal with (my dad was still alive then and was soon to be eighty-four years old). Rachel and I walked her down the aisle, standing as strong as we could under the circumstances.

The wedding was absolutely beautiful. We were two families of two different skin colors but both loving God with all of our hearts. To me, that was the most important thing—along with loving God with all our heart, soul, mind, and strength. Just like the sermon John preached two weeks before his death. I also remember what he said after Jeremy and Heather walked out of the house on their first date—"Red and yellow, black and white…They are precious in His sight." God does not look at the color of our skin. He looks at the heart.

There I was almost three years after John's death. Yes, I was still healing (and still am), but God reveals things to me every day. I have learned so much about God's word and have continued to trust in Him. I am reminded about the story of Job and how he trusted in God. Even though the devil was allowed to take everything away from him, he couldn't take his life.

God knew Job would never curse Him because he loved him with all his heart. Most of the chapters in the book of Job talks about how he lost everything (even his wife wanted him to curse God). His friends were also complaining about all that was happening to him and were telling him that he was doing something wrong to deserve all his troubles. Job wanted his friends to comfort him, not to make things worse. Job never sinned and never blamed God, but he did start complaining himself. He was then covered with boils, was scraping them with a piece of glass, and was wishing he had never been born.

He talks about how human life is a struggle. He talked about how he used to be respected in the community but then became the butt of everyone's jokes. He was beginning to wonder what he had done to deserve all that. He knew he hadn't done anything wrong and started questioning God, "Isn't disaster supposed to come those who do wrong?" He really felt he deserved a fair trial. The fear of the Lord had kept him from sinning, but he was confused as to why bad things were happening to him.

> In the 38th chapter, God would speak...Why do you confuse the issue? Why do you talk without knowing what you're talking about?...Were you

there when I created the earth?...Who decided on its size?...Who came up with the blueprints and measurements? How was its foundation poured, and who set the cornerstone, While the morning stars sang in chorus and all the angels shouted praise? And who took charge of the ocean when it gushed forth like a baby from the womb?...Have you ever gotten to the true bottom of things, explored the labyrinthe caves of deep ocean? Do you know the first thing about death? Do you have one clue regarding death's dark mysteries?...Do you know where Light comes from and where Darkness lives so you can take them by the hand and lead them home when they get lost?...Have you ever traveled to where snow is made, seen the vault where hail is stockpiled, the arsenals of hail and snow that I keep in readiness for times of trouble and battle and war? Can you find your way to where lightning is launched, or to the place from which the wind blows?...Do you know the first thing about the sky's constellations and how they affect things on Earth?...Can you teach the lioness to stalk her prey and satisfy the appetite of her cubs as they crouch in their den, waiting hungrily in their cave? And who sets out food for the ravens when their young cry to God, fluttering about because they have no food?... Are you the one who gave the horse his prowess and adorned him with a shimmering mane?...Did you command the eagle's flight, and teach her to build

> her nest in the heights perfectly at home on the high cliff face, invulnerable on pinnacle and crag?...Are you going to haul me, the Mighty One, into court and press charges? (Job 38–40, MSG)
>
> Job answered God: "You can do anything and everything. Nothing and no one can upset your plans. You asked, 'Who is this muddying the water, ignorantly confusing the issue, second-guessing my purposes?' I admit it. I was the one...You told me, 'Listen, and let me do the talking. Let me ask the questions. *You* give the answers.' I'm sorry—forgive me..." (Job 42:4, MSG)

Even Job had a difficult time while he was going through the fire. It is very hard to focus on anything when life slaps us in the face. I believe this story was written in the Bible to teach all of us something very powerful: Life will happen to all of us, but we all must listen when God speaks. He created all things and has everything under control. So when things look so bad and we don't think we can handle it, we must focus on the ever-loving, all-powerful God.

What an incredible and mighty God we serve! He is the omnipotent Father of mercy and grace. He is ever present, the creator of all things. He will never leave me or forsake me. He is all-knowing and all-powerful! He is ruler over all. He is the beginning and the end. He is the first and the last. He is my comforter, my strength, and my rock. He is my provider and in Him I put my trust. He is the author and finisher of my faith. He walks before me; and through Him, I can do all things. When I am weak, He becomes strong. When I can walk no further, He picks me up and carries me. Because of Him, I am never alone. Lord, if I seek You, I will find You; if I knock, You will open the door.

I have come to realize that God has a perfect plan for me. I may not know all the answers, but he does. Just like Job said, this human life is a struggle. The key is to trust in God and let Him do all the talking and ask all the questions. We have to believe that He is in total control of our lives.

I have learned so much since John's death. In such a short time, I went from having a family of four to living by myself, and what an adjustment it has been! I try to look for all the good in my life. The most important thing I have learned is trusting in God to comfort me. When things around me have faded or are gone and I feel everything has been stripped away, I find myself coming back to the heart of God in a way I have never known before. It has been a process—a day-by-day experience. Time may heal but God is the true healer.

The Bible talks about God being the husband to a widow, and I have found it to be so true. I have learned to find out what the Bible says and then stand firm on it. I know for a fact that I could have lost my mind had I chosen to go there, but God had given me the grace to live. Since I turned my mind over to Him, He has taken it, put positive words in it, and given me peace that surpasses all understanding. I don't know why things have to happen the way they do, but I do know God is in control.

The Bible says that trials will come. The important thing is that we equip ourselves with the truths of the Word so we become stronger each day. I cannot sit around every day worrying about what might happen to me or to my family. I have to put my trust in God to protect us from harm and danger. Sure, I have concerns about certain situations, but this is what I am talking about when I say He gives me a peace that passes all understanding. I can't explain it; I just believe it.

God has restored joy back into my life and has given me a love for people in a way I have never known. If I can speak words of life and encouragement to others, then my life will have been worth living. I have such a compassion for people who may not have experienced the love of Christ. I want them to find what's real in Him. I cannot imagine living life without Him, and I know He is *real.*

I still believe!

e|LIVE

listen|imagine|view|experience

AUDIO BOOK DOWNLOAD INCLUDED WITH THIS BOOK!

In your hands you hold a complete digital entertainment package. In addition to the paper version, you receive a free download of the audio version of this book. Simply use the code listed below when visiting our website. Once downloaded to your computer, you can listen to the book through your computer's speakers, burn it to an audio CD or save the file to your portable music device (such as Apple's popular iPod) and listen on the go!

How to get your free audio book digital download:

1. Visit www.tatepublishing.com and click on the e|LIVE logo on the home page.
2. Enter the following coupon code:
   279a-8a4a-f46d-e7ca-f290-7143-4c2a-a9d9
3. Download the audio book from your e|LIVE digital locker and begin enjoying your new digital entertainment package today!

CPSIA information can be obtained at www.ICGtesting.com
Printed in the USA
LVOW10s0601160916

504808LV00020B/98/P

9 781682 707685